He's the King,
But Girl You Are the Queen

Pastor R. J. Washington, Sr.

insight
PUBLISHING GROUP

Tulsa, Oklahoma

HE'S THE KING, BUT GIRL YOU ARE THE QUEEN

He's the King, but Girl You Are the Queen by R.J. Washington, Sr.
Published by Insight Publishing Group
8801 S. Yale, Suite 410
Tulsa, OK 74137
918-493-1718

Unless otherwise indicated, all Scripture quotations are from the King James Version of the Bible.

You have the author's permission to quote this book.

ISBN: 1-932503-02-1
Library of Congress Card Catalog number: 2003107491

Printed in the United States of America

Dedication

To God be all the glory, for the things, He has done
and honor to my Lord and Savior, Jesus Christ!

I dedicate this book to my beautiful wife,
April Washington,
whose smile has brought me much joy
over these past twenty-one years.

To my children, whom I love dearly:
Rodney Jr., Glorie and Titus

Contents

From the Father's Heart...

In the early '90's, God in His wisdom and great love, allowed me to see the spirit of divorce in a vision. Although, it was a demonic spirit, his appearance had an image of a bronze strong man. In the vision, he demonstrated great strength and power. He looked at me with a glare in his eyes. Then, an image of a brick house appeared which was very solid. Suddenly, he pointed his finger at the home, and the entire house exploded. Although it was a vision, it shook me up and I thought, *my God!*

Then, I heard a voice speak clearly unto me saying,

Son, this is the spirit of divorce, and he is destroying homes, and he is destroying families. I have an assignment for you. Your assignment is to heal and to build marriages. I am going to anoint you to minister to marriages, build marriages and bless marriages ... I am going to use you."

Satan, your adversary, will and plan is to destroy, bust up and tear down marriages and the unity of families. Although it seems that the devil has demonstrated great strength in your marriage and family, do you believe there *is* an answer from God? Although it may seem that satan has succeeded in sending an explosion to your home, do you believe there *is* an answer from God?

If your heart is still saying *yes*, then, there *is* a healing anointing to rebuild your marriage, your family and your home.

❧ *Prayer* ❧

God, heal and build the marriages of these individuals reading this book, as well as marriages everywhere. Forgive them of the mistakes that they have committed against you and one another. Nourish and mature them in their marriage. Prosper the crown of their marriage with a Godly love for each other. I decree a supernatural anointing of your love to fall fresh upon them now in Jesus name. Amen

Chapter One

I said, "I Do" ... But ...

You had a wedding, but do you have a marriage? Reality has set in, the bills are piling up, and there is less money. After counseling thousands of married couples, I have determined that the first years of marriage are the most *"trying"* times. If newly weds can endure through the first three years of marriage, they can make it. I refer to these years as the years of adjustment.

Why? The moment you say, **"I do", *you're through!*** You maybe saying, "How could you say such a thing?" Don't let the words, "I do, *you're through*" shock you. When a man and woman says, "I do" and are joined in holy matrimony, this literally means the *collision of two histories and lifestyles.*

Rather you were *shacking or courting* respectably "practicing abstinence"; now, you maybe saying, *"But ... we were better off before we said, I do."* Perhaps this is true. Nonetheless, now that you are attempting to do things according to God's word as it relates to marriage versus "shacking", satan's assignment of destruction for your relationship went to the next level of spiritual warfare.

Matthew 18:19-20,

Again, I say unto you, That if two of you shall agree on earth as touching any thing that they shall ask, it shall be done for them of my Father which is in Heaven. For where two or three are gathered together in my name, there am I in the midst of them.

When you were dating he was the kindest gentleman, and she was the sweetest young lady. *Dating is phony.* When you were dating, you were baiting her, and she was baiting you. He runs to open the car door and says, "Come right in, my sweet." He allows you to clear your dress, and then he closes the door for you. You are so impressed with his kindness that you tell your mother, "He's the nicest guy I've ever met." He's thinking, *"Oh when I get married..."*

Finally, you're married. Now they're saying, "Honey, are you going to open the door for me?" Your spouse looks at you and says, "Open the door yourself; what do you think this is, valet parking or something?"

While you were dating, if you tripped or stumbled over a curve, your spouse may ask, "are you alright, I'll sue the city!" Now that you are married, if you trip or stumble, they might say, "What's wrong with you?" Pick up your big feet, you're stumbling all over the place, hurry up, come on, can't you keep up!" The length of time you choose to "court" an individual is irrelevant; you may not get to know that person for who they really are until you are married.

The habits, problems or issues that are *within* a person before you marry, they will magnify; and in some cases, it's only going to get much worse. You have to allow God to intervene and work on him or her, through salvation and the *filling* of the Holy Ghost.

This is why it is so important to **first** seek God and marry in God's timing. The adjustment season is a little easier when you allow God to choose your mate. As with a natural King or Queen, when God chooses your spouse, He takes them through a preparation process *before* presenting them to you.

God, in His magnificent wisdom, has a preparation process that is totally contrary to mankind beliefs and process for marriage. We often believe the process starts when introduced to a person, that special eye contact, when you realize you have something "unique" in common or the first time your heart skips a beat when they say, "*I love you.*"

With God, the preparation process started when you were created and the desire was in you at this time.

Genesis 2:20-24 ,

But there was not an help meet for him. And the Lord God caused a deep sleep to fall upon Adam and he slept: and he took one of his ribs, and closed up the flesh instead thereof; And the rib, which the Lord God had taken from man, made he a woman, and brought her unto man. And Adam said, This is now bone of my bones, and flesh of my flesh: she shall be called Woman, because she was taken out of Man. Therefore shall a man leave his father and his mother, and shall cleave unto his wife: and they shall be one flesh.

Through childhood, adulthood, various situations and circumstances, men and women are being prepared for marriage. By the time you meet your mate, they should have something *very* significant and life changing to offer you, *spiritually* and naturally.

As you continue reading, you will learn more about diverse personalities. In order to help those of you that are married, separated, divorced and single, I want you to clearly understand that there are different personalities that make up a marriage.

For the single person waiting for God to manifest your husband or wife, please understand, just because an individual is saved and Holy Ghost filled, you are **not** automatically compatible. The two of you can both confess Christ and love the Lord with your whole heart, but if you don't have *anything* in common, then it is very possible that you are not compatible.

If you are as different as night and day, it's possible that you will argue constantly. God is the only one who can change mortality into immortality, incompatibility to compatibility. Unless God steps in and a *real breakthrough* occurs, that incompatible couple will have to *go through* to get to the place where God wants their marriage. *Ephesians 5:21-31,*

> *Submitting yourselves one to another in the fear of God. Wives, submit yourselves unto to your own husbands, as unto the Lord. For the husband is the head of the wife, even as Christ is the head of the church: and he is the saviour of the body. Therefore as the church is subject unto Christ, so let the wives be to their own husbands in every thing. Husbands, love your wives, even as Christ also loved the church, and gave himself for it: ... So ought men to love their wives as their own bodies. He that loveth his wife loveth himself ... For this cause shall a man leave his father and mother, and shall be joined unto his wife, and they two shall be one flesh.*

These are very encouraging words to help husbands and wives understand the way God desires the man to stand as the head of his house. However, many men have been lacking the knowledge to understand the responsibility of headship. It certainly doesn't mean that the man can abuse his authority and *"dog out"* his wife. Neither does it mean that the man has all the answers, or that you should not listen to your wife.

The real key to a strong marriage is when the husband and wife operate as a team, because it takes two. Equally, men and women, have a unique insight for certain situations. I don't care how spiritual you are; you won't know everything! God established an order, *husband, wife, children:* each spouse has a distinctive role. Therefore, respectfully, both the husband and the wife should manage certain areas within a home while moving together in harmony for a successful marriage.

Two are better than one; because they have a good reward for their labour. For if they fall, the one will lift up his fellow: but woe to him that is alone when he falleth: for he hath not another to help him up.
Ecclesiastes 4:9-10

❧❧

Chapter Two

Handle Your Business

God wants a harmonious flow in your marriage. God wants things to move and flow the way musical notes blend together to produce a beautiful melody, *Ephesians 5:19-20.* He desires for your marriage to operate at a steady pace in rhythm just like a band, marching in step and in sequence in the same direction.

It is very important for the man to understand his role in the marriage. His position is out front leading, as the head. The man is to a marriage what a drum major or director is to a band. In the Old Testament scriptures, God's original plan for man was to give him dominion and establish him as the **king, priest, prophet, judge, and ruler** of the home.

The system of family rule is referred to as patriarchal. That makes it extremely important for a man to know Jesus. Every man needs to be connected to Jesus as in accordance to *1 Corinthians 11:3, But I would have you know, that the head of every man is Christ; and the head of the woman is the man; and the head of Christ is God.*

Men, as the head of your house, you are to have the closest relationship with God. As the man, it is very difficult to lead your home effectively, without knowing Jesus Christ. Often times, the woman has a stronger relationship with God. The man has God's blessing and the obligation to fulfill his roles as the king, priest, prophet and judge.

As king, he sets up and establishes the order by which the home shall flow and the king delegates authority to the queen to ensure it is enforced. As the priest he leads prayer and keeps it flowing continually in his home. As a prophet, he speaks into the life of his wife and children. When rough situations occur and major decisions must be made, he is a judge.

The role of a wife is also very important. Many married women do not realize their *God* given responsibility as a *help meet*. *Genesis 2:20, And the Lord God said, It is not good that man should be alone; I will make him an help meet for him.* This means, *help meet* the car note, *help meet* the light bill, *help meet* the gas bill. I'm just teasing.

As the wife, God has given you the ability to manage your home. *Titus 2:5, To be discreet, chaste, keepers at home, good, obedient to their own husbands, that the word of God be not blasphemed.*

Many marriages operate and manage their financial affairs differently, in some marriages the husband is the best manager, in other cases, the wife. Which ever works best for your marriage, stick with it. Just make sure you pay your tithe and give an offering unto the Lord as commanded by God in *Malachi 3:8-12*, pay your bills and set aside some for a rainy day.

Mr. King, although these are acceptable forms of "entertainment" within the secular industry, **please don't** take the bill money and go to the casino, dog track or take your buddies out, when the bills are due. These "get rich quick" methods are ultimately damaging to you, your family and your relationship with God as it relates to **Godly** seed sowing. Also, you place an unnecessary burden on yourself by trying to play "catch up" the next month.

Likewise, Mrs. Queen, if the King has instructed you to use the credit card for emergencies only, don't purchase shoes and dresses and hide them in the back of the closet. When he finally notices your new wardrobe, you tell him, "Oh, this isn't new ... this old thing has been in the closet for a long time." Every month, you are constantly racing to the mailbox trying to keep him from seeing the credit card bills.

Marriage is not a business, but there is a business side to it. You must strive to be fervent in business as a couple. If you are having problems in this area, consider creating a monthly budget and set goals to reduce your debts. Keep your entertainment expenses to a minimum, when the income is low. In today's society, convenience is now a necessity. Nonetheless, if you must cut the "cable television", cut it! When possible, try to resist compulsive or unbudgeted spending. Remember, *"same as cash"* is really delayed debt with a *huge* interest rate.

Contrary to many opinions, sex is not the greatest problem within most marriages. Some of the greatest problems within a family today are really due to financial situations. Money cannot pay your way to heaven and it cannot pay your way out of hell. Nor can money buy genuine love, but when the money is not right everything else starts falling apart. No matter how you say, "I love you baby girl, I love you so and I never want to let you go!" Brother, if you ask your wife to spell love, she may say, love is spelled, "m-o-n-e-y!"

Financial stability is a key component. As a man, you are expected to have *consistent* income. You may hate your work environment, but it is important to report to work on time and perform your best. Constantly, quitting your job or being fired for poor performance is not stability. This also places an unnecessary burden on your wife and children. Honestly, I know that caring for a *"queen"* in today's economy is not cheap! As a man, do your very best to take care of your wife. God requires you to provide for her and your children. *1 Timothy 5:8, But, if any provide not for his own, and specially for those of his own house, he hath denied the faith, and is worse than an infidel.*

During premarital counseling, I constantly encourage couples to pray by touching and agreeing concerning how to handle the financial and business part of their marriage, whatever the decision, stick to it. Each person must know their strengths and weaknesses. Once, both of you agree that the money will be handled a certain way, don't change your mind. You shouldn't get away from the original plan, especially, not without the agreement of your spouse.

Chapter Three

Is it in the Right Hands?

I often use the fivefold ministry gifts of the church in relation to marriages. The order by which God has established for the church is very similar to the setup God wants for the family unit. By using your hand, you can remember the fivefold ministry gifts: apostle (thumb), prophet (index finger), evangelist (middle finger), pastor (wedding ring finger), and teacher (pinky finger).

The thumb can touch every finger on the hand, much like the apostle who can touch every ministry gift. The apostle has the ability to establish churches as well as pastor a church. He can evangelize an area and establish another church, or he can help with missions. The apostle is defined as the *"sent one,"* or *"one sent by God."* In other words, the apostle was sent to do what Jesus would have done if He were still in the flesh. The apostle is equipped with special gifting to do certain things and a lot of people will have to take notice of it. An apostle can do something in three years that it would take a regular pastor twenty years to accomplish.

The prophet, the index finger. He points prophetically and speaks, *"Yea, thus saith the Lord..."*

The evangelist, the longest finger on your hand, is the one that performs the outreach and the spreading of the good news of Jesus Christ, *"We Love You to Life."*

The ring finger is the pastor. He is committed to the ministry and his commitment is to prepare the bride, *the church* for the coming of her bridegroom, *Jesus Christ.*

The smallest finger on your hand represents the ministry of the teacher. He instructs, directs and informs.

You can really build and strengthen your marriage by using your hand to describe the five basic areas in your marriage.

The thumb represents LOVE. With love, you can touch every area of your marriage. The thumb can touch every finger on your hand. Likewise, the fingers on your hand represent other vital areas of your marriage, when touched by your thumb, *love*, enhances that area in your marriage. *Ephesians 5:25, Husbands love your wives even as Christ also loved the church and gave himself for it.*

This commandment alone has more weight than basically anything that God tells the woman to do. God tells the man, I want you to love your wife just like I love the church. That's a "deep" love. In other words, if you can not love her like I love the church, you *don't* deserve her. If you can not love her the way Christ loves the church, you should *not* marry her. If you do not have that kind of love, you are not going to respect her. You will not treat her as royalty.

What will Jesus do for the church? Jesus loves me and you so much, that He died on the cross for our sins. **That's a great love!**

The index finger represents the COMMUNICA-TION area of the marriage. It's so important to have an open line of communication at all times in your marriage. Many times husbands and wives do very little communicating. If you think back in your minds to the countless hours the two of you spent talking to each other on the phone when you were dating and courting, you will realize that the amount of conversations you have now is far less than when you were courting. Now that you're married, you can easily point at, and point out things that are not right. When the thumb touches the index finger, when love touches communication, you begin to speak to one another differently.

Do not use words that will hurt each other; these things will cause serious damage to your trust. Remember, your thumb represents love; you must have a touch of love in your communication towards each other. Don't let anyone fool you, words carry a spiritual power. Positive words build, compliment and encourage, but negative words are destructive, demeaning and they hurt. You can never take back negative words that are spoken irrationally or out of anger.

I always tell married couples to *never* speak the word "divorce". Do not tell your spouse you want a divorce during a heated disagreement. Sometimes arguments will occur. *Teeth and tongue will fall out.* When you are angry you might say things to hurt one another, but don't say the word divorce out loud, because some words have power and a spirit is connected to it, *Proverbs 6:2, "Thou art snared with the words of thy mouth, thou art taken with the words of thy mouth."*

Ephesians 4:26, "Be ye angry, and sin not: let not the sun go down upon your wrath." If the situation gets too uncontrollable, walk away or seek counseling, from a Godly man or woman. God does not condone, or tolerate that type of behavior. *"Let not the sun go down on your wrath"* means, do not let the situation continue all day and into the night. You must control your anger and settle disagreements quickly, when possible. Don't allow the devil to take advantage of a situation and escalate it. One of the fruits of the spirit is temperance, which is self control, *Galatians 5:23.*

Your marriage is literally built on words. Words that are fulfilled, performed, spoken and carried out. It's also built on misused words that were not carried out. Words misused in anger often will chip away from the love, and bring dullness and staleness to your marriage. Those little words you speak out of your mouth can either build your marriage or gradually destroy it. When your marriage becomes dry you will wonder whatever happened to the freshness and the newness you once shared in the beginning of your marriage.

Every one of us has feelings and various needs in our marriage. Considering your spouse's feelings and needs causes your marriage to grow to a different level of maturity. Everybody has a soft spot that can be touched. If you're married to a person for any length of time, you know where their soft spot is located. You know exactly what to say to tear them down and hit them where it hurts. Man, you know exactly what to say to make tears stream down a woman's cheek. Sometimes when people say certain things, it's because they are speaking out of their own hurt, like a wounded, bleeding, ferocious bear. *Proverbs 15:1 says, "A soft answer turneth away wrath: but grievous words stir up anger."*

Remember, your words are important. Use words that compliment and encourage her, and be genuine. I know that most men use three or four of these words to express how much they love their wives. Words like darling, honey, baby, sweetie, angel, dear, beautiful, sugar pie or cutie pie. Some may like to be called, *"Sugar*

Bear." Don't try that, I'm just teasing. Her self-esteem and her confidence will rise just because of your words. The words you say to her really show how you feel about her. Say kind and gentle words to her that make her feel special. This will increase the longevity of your marriage.

Men enjoy compliments as well. Stroke his ego with words like, handsome, you're the man, my baby and you are the greatest. If you learn to feed a man's ego, he will become the *dimeless prophet*; he'll go broke trying to please you. If you start telling that man how wonderful he is, he won't be able to take it. His confidence and self-esteem will rise just like the woman. Then tell him, "Ooh baby, I am going to take good care of you tonight." *That will make him crazy.* He will give you every dime in his pocket. You'll be smiling and he'll be broke.

Take time and hear your spouse's heart. You may hear them say, "I really want you to be my protector, and my inspector. I want you to be right here for me. I want you to back me up. I want you to treat me with respect. I want you to love me like you have never loved me before."

The longest finger on your hand represents the FINANCES of the marriage. I can not reiterate this enough; in many cases the divorce rate is so high, due to poor money management. Many marriages end in divorce, because couples fail to properly plan. Unfortunately, divorce is higher in the church than in the world. I want you to remember that, in many instances, you must treat your marriage as a business. A good business strategy to remember for your marriage is, *"if you fail to plan, then you plan to fail."* Many times when I minister on marriage, I will define the word divorce as, "the marriage has gone out of business." Much like a business that goes out of business and sells all its remaining assets, similarly, divorces cause couples to sell and divide furniture, cars, property and even separate the children in some cases.

If you are not giving your tithes and offerings, then you are hindering yourself and your family. When you are obedient and operate in the area that God ordained for His church: blessings will flow *on you and to you.* Likewise, when you operate in what God has ordained in your marriage the blessings **will** follow you.

The ring finger in the marriage represents the SEXUAL area. In some marriages, in terms of importance, it represents about *10* percent. Other couples it may represent *25* percent or more; it varies with different couples. This is also the most sensitive area of the marriage. Sex is a gift that God gave you to share with one another, as husband and wife. If you refuse to satisfy your husband then how will he be satisfied? When possible, make every attempt to attend to his special needs.

I often tell men in wisdom, that if your wife works as many hours as you, don't expect her to come home from work, attend to the needs of your children, clean, cook, and satisfy you sexually all night. Husband, consider helping with the chores and try to understand that her body goes through many changes, physically and emotionally.

Fatigue, allows for tempers, tension, and anger to creep in your marriage. When your spouse is tired don't begin to beat them with scripture or religiosity. **Caution!** Remember, too little sex is dangerous and too much can be dangerous; *don't wear your gift out.*

The pinky finger represents the area of TRUST. "DON'T' BETRAY THE TRUST WITHIN YOUR MARRIAGE!" Man, you're a dead man if you loose your wife's trust. A woman literally uses both sides of her brain and a man only uses one side of his brain. A woman has the ability to retain more detailed information than a man. The Holy Ghost never forgets God's Word. He will lead and guide you into all truth and he will bring all things back to your remembrance. Guess what, so will a woman.

I said that humorously. Nonetheless, every man and woman can remain faithful. Rather you're on your job, at church or vacationing, don't allow yourself to be placed in a compromising position where you *can* entertain sin. Should you find yourself in an uncomfortable situation and your heart starts doing flips when a particular woman is in your presence and you like her, the devil is tempting you. Your heart is doing flips because the devil knows your type of woman. Believe me; the devil knows what looks good to every man and every woman. He also knows exactly what it will take for you to yield to sin. In fact, the devil has been tempting and baiting you for years. He has studied and memorized your appetite. He is not going to bring you an onion sandwich when he knows you like a steak sandwich.

The devil also tempts precious women, the same way. Women, you have to know that when you are around a certain man on the job and your heart starts doing flips, the devil is tempting you. Let me paint a scenario for you. You are home with your insensitive husband, who never compliments you. You are wearing the same old pink robe he bought you for an anniversary gift three years ago. You know, the one that has the cotton curling up like knots and your husband comes over and says to you, "Take that old robe off!" One day while you are at work minding your own business, a new man comes into the work area, notices you and begins to compliment you. He says, "Oh girl, you look good; any man would be blessed to have you." The next day, he says, "I like the way you wear your hair." A woman is vulnerable to compliments. Compliments make them feel special or like a queen. Husband, it's your job to keep her smothered and covered with compliments and sweet words.

Men cheat on their wives for sex, and many women cheat for love, affection, and compliments. The devil loves to plant seeds that sow the spirit of division in a vulnerable mind. He says, "You deserve better treatment than what you've been getting from them." If that thought continues to fester in a persons mind, the devil planted it successfully and eventually the vulnerable spouse will yield to the temptation.

Why is it that you can laugh with everyone else except your spouse? When you go home you're mad with your wife? The two of you haven't laughed in months. Man, you can laugh with other females but you can't laugh with your wife. Woman, you find yourself able to laugh with other men or brothers in Christ, and you feel so happy and free but you cannot laugh with your own husband.

You better check it before you wreck it! Your best friend is your spouse, like Batman and Robin or Bonnie and Clyde.

Chapter Four

Single, but Not Alone

Many of you have endured a very traumatic situation called divorce. Some of you are recipients of cruelty and were left with the short end of the stick. However, before you can start courting again you must release that other person out of your heart. You are probably still very angry over what happened in the past and have not forgiven your ex-spouse. Others of you are still in love and don't understand why the entire divorce occurred. There is nothing wrong with you for feeling that way about your ex-spouse. For some of you, God will restore your marriage and bring you back together. In the meantime, you *must* follow God and do it *His* way, because *you maybe single but you are not alone.*

You may have fasted, prayed, consecrated, and sought the face of God fervently and they still left. It's hard, it's tough, but the only way to go forward is to let go of the past. Before you make plans to marry again, be sure that he or she is completely out of your heart. Perhaps both of you were partly to blame or they were completely wrong. Deep in your heart, you are still in love. You love them so much, if they confronted you right now, you would fall head over hills in love again. But, they have moved on with their life and you have *got* to do the same by letting go of the past. When you really release the memories of the past and the good times you had together, you will be able to move on with your life.

An example of a person who has not completely released another person is when there are biblical scriptures to support the divorce. They continue to believe God for restoration while remaining miserable day after day and year after year. For instance, a woman is dating "Billy Bob", but often while in conversation with him, her mind wonders back to thoughts of "Jerry". She begins to tell Bob about how she remembers an incident that happened when Jerry came by to visit her.

She says, "I remember it was during Christmas season, and Jerry had on a cute red sweater, blue jeans and those nice sneakers we purchased from the mall on our summer vacation. He came into the house and said, "I have something for you." His hands were behind his back. He pulled out a water gun and squirted me with it." She laughs while saying, "I was soaked." While reminiscing to Bob about her "fun" memories of Jerry, Bob just looks at her. Then he says, "If you say one more thing about Jerry, I can't take this anymore!" Bob recognizes that Jerry is still in her heart and he realizes that there is no room for him. He cannot have an effective relationship with her because she needs to "get over" Jerry.

If she would allow God to heal her, she could release the memories, desires and break free from the **"Soul Ties"** of Jerry. They shared some bad times in the past. The memories of those experiences are erased from her mind because she is still *"in love"*, and the tragic situation is forgotten. **"Soul Ties"** have blinded the reality of the tragic situation which caused the current situation.

Divorce is the death of a marriage. I know that it is tough for you now that it is over. I also know that at times it maybe difficult to make it through a day. If you have taken the time to read this book, there **is** enough strength and determination within you to get on with your life, follow God and do it His way.

God is going to send you someone who will love you and your life will never be the same. Your life will change but in the meantime, I want to encourage you to remember these three words, *Get Over It!* In order for you to go on with your life, you *must* release the hurt, anger, frustrations and memories out of your heart. Just, *"let it go."* As difficult and as painful as it maybe, the only way to go forward is to let go of the past. God still has a plan and purpose with great things for your life. Someday, soon, you will be someone's king or queen.

You maybe saying, "So what do I do now Pastor. I am already divorced with children. I did not deserve to get a divorce. I did my part; it was their fault. They allowed themselves to be used by the devil. They were so rebellious and wouldn't listen. Now my children's lives are on the line. What do I do in this case?"

First, stop blaming yourself and take those children to God in prayer. You must begin the healing and rebuilding process with your children. As painful as it may be to you, you must explain it to them from your heart and not out of your emotions. Continue to pray that God will open their understanding about the events that led to the divorce. Do all that you can to make their lives as fulfilling and as holistic as you possibly can. Continue to love them and build up their self-esteem and teach them to love God.

Continue to reassure your children that they can talk to you anytime. You must go the extra mile in reaching out to them in a special way by loving them unconditionally. Meaning, love them without any strings attached. Finally, be very selective, in whom you allow your children to interact and socialize with at all times. Always know their daily activities. Protect, respect and nurture them. You do the possible and God will do the impossible.

❧ Prayer ❧

Heavenly Father we ask, in Jesus name, that you would touch the heart of this man or woman. I pray that first, their love and relationship with you will be restored. Because of the hurts of the past, they are looking for someone to blame. This hurt has caused them to turn from you, Lord.

Father I pray that they would ask for your forgiveness, and allow you to come back into their hearts and heal them of the hurts of the past. Fill that empty spot with your love, peace and joy.

Father we intercede right now for the children. God cover them, you said, that you would be a Father to the fatherless. Wrap your loving arms around these children and embrace them like only you can. Give this parent, new wisdom to continue to raise these children.

Father, manifest your Glory in their lives. We know that they maybe single but they are not alone because they have you. Amen.

Chapter Five

The Past, The Present, Our Future

Deuteronomy 30:19, I call heaven and earth to record this day against you, that I have set before you life and death, blessing and cursing; therefore choose life, that both thou and thy seed may live.

God wants you to choose life in your marriage, because He wants you and your seed to live. The decisions that you make in your marriage are going to directly affect your children. This is very important. Do not let anyone fool you. You have everything to do with the outcome of the success of your children. This is not to say that they won't rebel against you, make some crazy choices, and just choose to do things their own way, but a healthy marriage will influence the outcome of your children and their choices in a more positive manner.

Many of us, as we look at our sons and daughters; they look just like their parents. In most cases, daughters resemble their mothers and sons resemble their fathers. Oftentimes, the children act like their parents. How many times have you said, "*You act just like your father or you act just like you mother.*"

Although it's just a similarity, what you are really seeing is the manifestation of curses being passed down from generation to generation. God says, he wants you to choose life and not death and He wants you to choose a blessing and not a curse. I am glad that I accepted Jesus Christ into my life at the age of sixteen and I have remained faithful to Jesus Christ because I love him. Also, I desire to continue my walk with God because it will have a greater bearing on my children. If you are enticed into any type sin, that spirit and possibly many others will fall upon your children. You are shaping a pattern for your children's future. However, once you receive Christ, the *buck stops right there*! Because, you accepted Jesus Christ into your life, the curse is broken!

I am speaking of generational curses that will follow from one generation to the next generation. *Exodus 20:5, Thou shalt not bow down thyself to them, nor serve them: for I the Lord thy God am a jealous God, visiting the iniquity of the fathers upon the children unto the third and fourth generations of them that hate me.*

You can live in Moscow, Russia, Germany or California and the curse will still fall on your seed in Jacksonville, Florida or wherever they maybe living. You must understand that the devil cannot be everywhere at the same time but he releases other demonic spirits; one will attack the father because his sins create an open door for other demonic spirits to enter. The other spirits will attack his sons and daughters. The military could send you overseas, and the sins you committed thousand of miles over the ocean will find you out! Your sins and those spirits which are **now** attached to you *or that are dwelling within you,* will follow you to your home. Their ultimate destination is your children. The same spirit that tempted and attacked you will also attack them.

The attacks upon your sons or daughters will occur earlier than the time when you were attacked. By the time they reach the actual age you were when you committed the sin, that spirit would have already oppressed them. They won't know or understand why they are addicted to a particular sin, *but there is good news!*

As a child of God, you have the authority to plead the **blood of Jesus** and to proclaim that the buck stops right here. You must get determined in your spirit, and demand in the name of Jesus Christ that the generational curses will not come on your seed! Begin speaking blessings and not curses, exercising your authority by standing on the Word and watching God perform His Word for you.

Even now, as you **plead the blood** over your family and speak blessings and not curses, everything that you have been experiencing has to be reversed. There is hope for you. There is **no** situation too hopeless for God. After receiving Christ, you do not want to backslide and reactivate the curse. Even though certain sins happened before you received Jesus Christ, you still need to constantly **plead the blood of Jesus** and stand against that situation by speaking life and not death. *Death in this perspective means, negative and unfruitful words.*

Use your rightful authority and those demonic spirits assigned to your children will have to *back off*. God is recording every word that you speak. How many records have you stored in heaven that are actual prayers prayed over the lives of your children? Your prayers will follow them the remainder of their days. Are you willing to pay the price by entering into your home and doing some maintenance? You must pay a price to maintain your marriage and family.

During premarital and marital counseling, I minister to couples in a special way regarding marriage and children. Oftentimes, because couples are "*so in love*", they agree and answer "*yes*" to everything. I always include the following:

In addition to caring for a new wife, are you prepared to provide for children from a previous marriage or relationship; and Are you willing to do your very best to work with the children's biological father or mother and befriend them so that everything can flow smoothly?

Of course the answers are always, *"I'm willing and Yes."* You must clearly understand that the responsibility of marrying someone with and without children is totally different.

You must consider the legal aspects of the custody agreement. Are you attempting to nurture your children in a Godly environment? If so, you must consider how it will affect you when the biological parent, who has joint custody, is not a Christian.

When the child is away visiting the other parent, they may permit them do certain things you have not approved, rather its secular music, cable television or dating. When the child returns into your home there will be spiritual and natural conflicts. Now you must confront the situation with a different approach. These are just some of the things you must consider.

It is important to stay in agreement with your spouse during challenging times regarding the children. If not, there rebellion will work against you by trying to destroy your marriage. Children know how to manipulate situations and come between the two of you. Children are much wiser now than when we were twelve and thirteen years old. A lot of us were watching cartoons; they grew out of that at age, six. They not only know how to get directly in the middle of your marriage but they know how to get what they want.

As parents, you should agree how to handle certain situations. You must show love, but *not* appear weak to them. When children determine a weakness or sense that you are not in agreement, they will continue to "add friction" to that particular situation. Let them know that both of you are in complete agreement about your decision. They will try to get a "yes" answer from their biological parent, when the stepparent, says, "no." Then, you and your spouse are arguing over a "control issue", failing to realize that the child manipulated the argument.

The parent that has shared custody may also try to manipulate the children by saying, "I'm your real father, and if he puts his hands on you, I will kill him!" This is not right. These situations must be addressed quickly because it places the "stepparent" in a terrible and uncomfortable situation.

I use the term "stepparent" with much reservation. Personally, I do not believe in the term "stepparent" and it's not biblical. When a couple says, "I do", the "stepparent" assumes the role of a parent by making the same sacrifices.

As a husband, you are the head of your household. When you marry someone with children, you are to help discipline and keep the children in their respectful place. As a wife, you and the children must respect your husband's authority in the house.

If you are not willing to submit to your husband's leadership regarding the children, you should not marry. If you are married, guess what, *it's too late.*

Scripturally, God requires you to submit to the leadership of your husband ... if not ... woe be unto you ...
eventually your children will rebel against you.

Ultimately, the parent residing with the child must
explain to the children that the new parent is also their
parent. They should honor and respect them as their parent. The two of you must explain to the children that this
relationship is very serious. When I counsel children, I
help them through the adjustment period by being honest. The child may say, "I already have a daddy or
mommy, I don't need another one." My answer is,
"you're going to have two and you will respect both of
them. All of you are a family."

Oftentimes the new spouse or the children are
experiencing many different emotions. Some children feel
frightened or fearful of being forced out of the house by
the new parent. They have grown accustom to having all
of the attention. Now, they must share the love and vice
versa. The new parent may think that the spouse only
cares about the children. In spite of the situation, as husband and wife, you must spend time together to build
your relationship. With God's help, you must continue
to press *and pray* through every situation. Never consider
separation or divorce as an option when the adjustment
period lasts longer than you may expect.

I strongly believe that a married couple should stay
together because of the children and not divorce. I really
mean that and I won't take it back. I won't back down
from making such a **bold** statement. You're probably say-

ing, "*you must want me miserable?*" No, I don't desire anyone to be miserable, that is not the will of God. However,
I often consider the lasting affect a divorce has upon a
child. A divorce is devastating to children, especially
when they are young. Honestly, the age of the child is
irrelevant when a divorce occurs; they will be affected in
one way or another for the rest of their lives.

They never really understand why mommy and
daddy are not together. They always question within
themselves. *Where is my mommy? Where is my daddy?* They
often blame themselves. "Did we do something to make
it happen?" "Was it our fault that the marriage did not
make it?" Many of them will become torn.

According to statistics, children of divorce are easily drawn to street life. The reason is they are yearning for
affection and attention. When the first person reaches
out and shows affection and attention, that person will
win them over. Unfortunately, this person could possess
a homosexual, lesbian and many other ungodly spirits.

For these reasons and if you are experiencing marital problems, it is important to seek Godly counseling
when the situation begins. Do not be afraid to get help.
There is nothing wrong with getting counseling. Or as
added assurance, ask your Pastor to pray and "*touch and
agree*" with you for your marriage to grow strong in the
name of Jesus. Remember, God is concerned about everything that concerns you, *the past, present and future.*

Chapter Six

Take it to the Throne

Blessed is the man that walketh not in the
counsel of the ungodly, nor standeth in the way
of sinners, nor sitteth in the seat of the scornful.
Psalm 1:1

I cannot fully express the importance of Godly counseling and it is *very* important to make the house of God your **first choice**. When a marriage is experiencing hurt and a couple requires counseling, *one* major ingredient for the first stage of counseling is required; a neutral party who knows God's word, has the Holy Ghost and who can get a prayer through to God.

When considering counseling, **don't** wait until the problems become so severe and divorce is a seed planted and growing rapidly in your heart, mind and manifesting on paper by an attorney. A lot of times the man is the last one to realize that there is *a* problem. When he finally realizes that the problems in his home are very serious, it is often too late, although many times the warning signs are very evident. The woman cries out for help, but when reality hits, the husband often says, "I didn't know the problem was *this* severe." The problem was there all the time and the wife was crying out, over and over again regarding certain areas. Sometimes, there are things that men just simply overlook. Unfortunately, when the situation reaches this stage in a marriage, the wife seeks to share her heart with just about anyone who will listen attentively, *male or female.*

Therefore, it is very important **not** to discuss your problems with relatives and friends unless they are anointed to help you and willing to keep everything you discuss confidential. You may feel very close to a cousin, sister or aunt and you may think you can share your marital problems with them. Oftentimes, couples share their problems with relatives not expecting them to gossip about the situation. It's not always wise to tell Uncle Joe or Auntie Sue.

After Uncle Joe or Auntie Sue tells the story to Cousin Leola and it continues its way through your family, your spouse is pictured as a "big bad wolf or demon". When the two of you repent and resolve your issues, your family members picture you as a "fool". This is why it is very important to take your cares, hurts, children and spouse to the throne of God. **Prayer still changes things!**

You must also understand that not everyone is praying to God for your marriage to last. You do not need old wise tales and tricks about how to "keep" your husband or wife. Some people whom you may admire and trust such as relatives, friends, co-workers, and many others will tell you to do certain things or tricks to "keep them". The devil is a liar! The Spirit of God will show you how to love and keep your spouse.

Believe it or not there are people that operate in witchcraft and they continually pray to the devil against marriages. They chant certain names of married couples, and place their names on *their* altar, just as Christians put names on the Holy altar. They present these names to satan and ask him to destroy that marriage.

Witches hire people to help them destroy marriages in Hollywood. They collect magazine articles to obtain the names and pictures of Hollywood stars. They pray and present sacrifices to the devil, and will do whatever it takes to destroy that marriage. Then after so many months, those marriages will begin to crumble, because they *are not* built on the foundation of Jesus Christ.

I feel compelled to share this true story with you. There were two ladies traveling on a plane. The airline stewardess offered them food and beverages, they replied, "We don't want any food. Right now, the two of us are fasting to the devil. Marriages in every city that this plane flies across will be terminated, destroyed and wiped out. We are fasting to satan to destroy marriages because we are witches."

These witches were fasting to the devil. They were not eating any food because they desired the devil to break up marriages. If you don't think you have a force working against your marriage, *you are wrong!* To fight against this force, it takes you and your spouse getting on "one accord" in prayer to God, Jesus and the Holy Ghost. You must *touch and agree* regularly by taking your cares to the throne of God.

Always remember, as King and Queen, the last voice speaking to the King is the Queen. She is the last one to speak *encouragement, motivation and sweet words* into his life before the day ends. Also, the Queen's ear should be attentive to hear as the King speaks *life, vision and direction* into her spirit as well ... and always remember ... **God hears both of you.**

Chapter Seven

As Royalty, I Require More

As a pastor, for the past eighteen years, I have determined that husbands and wives often fail to recognize the needs of their mate. To keep a marriage healthy and happy, it requires you to become more sensitive to the needs of one another, while understanding that your desires are vastly different.

Men need sexual fulfillment but women require more than sex. Women desire affection and compliments and if the husband gives her what she rightfully deserves, she will fulfill your sexual desires with a *glad heart*.

Communication is not only a requirement but a necessity for a woman. Husband, many times you must allow your wife to honestly and openly express herself. *Let her get it all out; it may take two hours, but that's your wife.* Women like to express themselves. You have to give her free course to talk. She has to vocalize her emotions. She needs to express how she feels, and what's bothering her and how you can be the solution to the problem. She needs to be able to release what's in her heart and share it with you.

Wives, your husband needs a recreational companion. Having your support when he wants to "shoot a few hoops", go bowling or golfing with the guys is important to him. He needs to know that you are *backing him up* instead of criticizing or *nagging* him. If women would remove the "*mask*" for a moment, they could see how selfish they really are at times, in this area. Women, your husbands need to know that you are supporting them even when they are not in your presence.

Husband, when you are having fun and she's at home with the small children, be considerate of the time. Try to come home at the time you both have agreed upon and flow with the arrangement. She needs to feel respected, valued and trusted.

I completely understand that you may not agree with this next suggestion, but it's important to your wife and *I am sure she will agree*, spend some time with her at the mall. Shopping makes her feel good, and having you with her makes it even better. Shop and walk around the mall with her. She will feel like a queen because you are *backing her up.*

Husband, your wife wants you to desire her. Picking at her cellulite can bore a hole in her psychologically and she will literally close up, mentally, physically and spiritually. When its time for bed, you will wonder, "why is she wearing an astronaut suit to bed?" Your criticism has caused her to feel shameful of her body.

Both of you should spend more time pampering one another on a regular basis. King, hold and cuddle your Queen tightly. Queen, rub and massage his feet and back. King, you should do the same to her ... and ... go to sleep ... *if you can...*

From the Pastor's Heart

Time is at hand; God wants to heal and build your marriage. If you really want God to heal your marriage you must be absolutely honest and open with God and yourself. Confess your faults one to another before God, repenting of your mistakes, anger, deception and lies. Jesus is faithful to forgive you of your mistakes. You have got to forgive others, and yourself. Do not hold on to the guilt. Repent of your mistakes and cast away the guilt. "Repent", in the words of Jesus, means, *"go and sin no more."* Do not willfully and knowingly predestinate, forecast, plot, predict, premeditate, or plan to commit sin.

Although Jesus is faithful to forgive you when you repent, your repentance must be from your heart, and **never** again knowingly commit or entertain that sin. Now that you understand true repentance, take your spouse by the hand and pray this prayer together in faith with a sincerity and God will hear and honor your requests.

❧ Prayer ❧

Oh God, heal the hurt and distrust in this marriage. I'm asking you to forgive us as we repent before you of our mistakes. Oh God, we come before you now, in the name of Jesus, confessing all of our sins and mistakes that we have made in our marriage. We confess that we have not loved one another like your Word says.

We, confess that we have not kept our marital vows that we made before you. Forgive us now, oh Lord, for the bitterness, anger, backbiting, and for sharing our problems with other family members and friends without coming to you and allowing you to work it out through prayer and Godly counseling. I pray that the love we shared for each other returns right now.

I pray for a restoration and revival of love in my marriage. Bind us together again in love. We confess that Jesus Christ is the head of our marriage. Save our marriage in Jesus name. Amen.

National Prayer Covering

Father, in the name of Jesus, I pray for those separated from their spouse. If they would release the past, you said that you would restore their marriages. God, heal and restore life, health and strength back into their marriage. Father, I pray that these marriages will have honesty, communication and sexual fulfillment. Thank you for these marriages that have been blessed by the revelations you have given me in this book. I rebuke the spirit of divorce and every demon that attacks marriages: disunity, dysfunctional spirits, unfaithfulness, adultery and every pornographic spirit. I rebuke every spirit that is not like you. Oh God, I pray that your hand would intervene in every situation. I rebuke wedges that separate and divide marriages. Sometimes relatives will come between a husband and wife, I pray that they would have a clear conscience towards one another by realizing what they do and say. Thank you for insight and wisdom. I pray for a *"break through"* to take place in these marriages. Where the honey has dripped out, put the honey back into the moon! Build up these marriages! Bless and heal in the sexual areas that have been a struggle in their bodies. Properly, restore the intimacy within the woman and man. Bless the finances of those that are obedient to your Word concerning tithe and offerings. Send an increase that will rain upon their finances. Bless the area of trust in their marriage. Let the man become more affectionate by speaking soft words to his wife. Let him talk to his wife as when they were dating by saying sweet things to her and not words that will tear her down. Bless the wife to meet the needs of her husband with sexual fulfillment and as a recreational companion. God, build him up so he is not torn down as a man. Help them to build their future and other families. Father, I pray this prayer of faith from my heart in Jesus' precious name. Amen.

Author Contact Information

Titus Harvest Dome Spectrum Church

10551 Beach Boulevard

Jacksonville, Florida 32246

(904) 646-9991